D0382062

FIRST GRAPHICS

MY COMMUNITY

GOING TO THE DENTIST

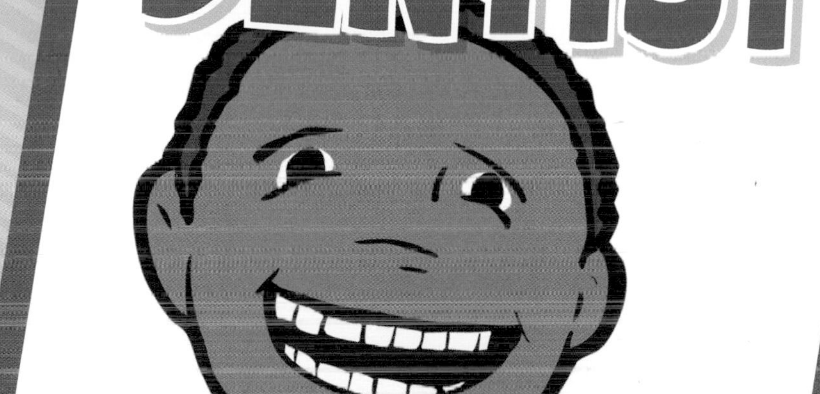

BY LORI MORTENSEN

ILLUSTRATED BY JEFFREY THOMPSON

Consultant: Judith R. Chin DDS, MS
Associate Professor, Department of Pediatric Dentistry
Indiana University, Indianapolis

CAPSTONE PRESS
a capstone imprint

First Graphics are published by Capstone Press,
151 Good Counsel Drive, P.O. Box 669, Mankato, Minnesota 56002.
www.capstonepub.com

For information regarding permission, write to Capstone Press,
151 Good Counsel Drive, P.O. Box 669, Dept. R, Mankato, Minnesota 56002.
Printed in the United States of America in Stevens Point, Wisconsin.

032010
005741WZF10

Library of Congress Cataloging-in-Publication Data
Mortensen, Lori.
    Going to the dentist / by Lori Mortensen ; illustrated by Jeffrey Thompson.
       p. cm.—(First graphics. My community)
    Summary: "In graphic novel format, text and illustrations describe a visit to the
dentist"—Provided by publisher.
    Includes bibliographical references and index.
    ISBN 978-1-4296-4507-2 (library binding)
    ISBN 978-1-4296-5610-8 (paperback)
    1. Dentistry—Comic books, strips, etc—Juvenile literature. I. Title. II. Series.
    RK63.M67 2011
    617.6'01—dc22
                                                                                    2009051473

Editor: **Erika L. Shores**
Designer: **Alison Thiele**
Art Director: **Nathan Gassman**
Production Specialist: **Laura Manthe**

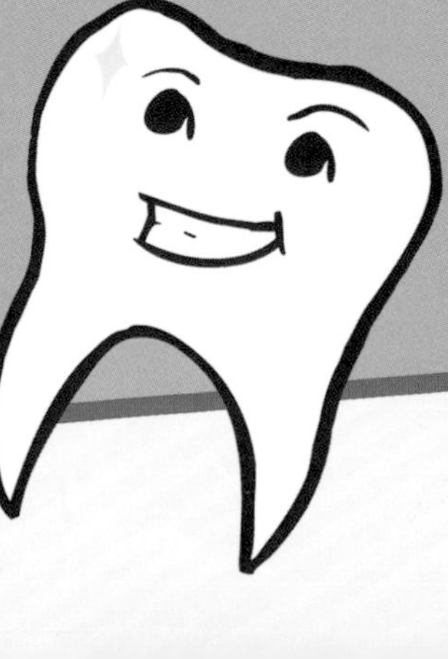

TABLE OF CONTENTS

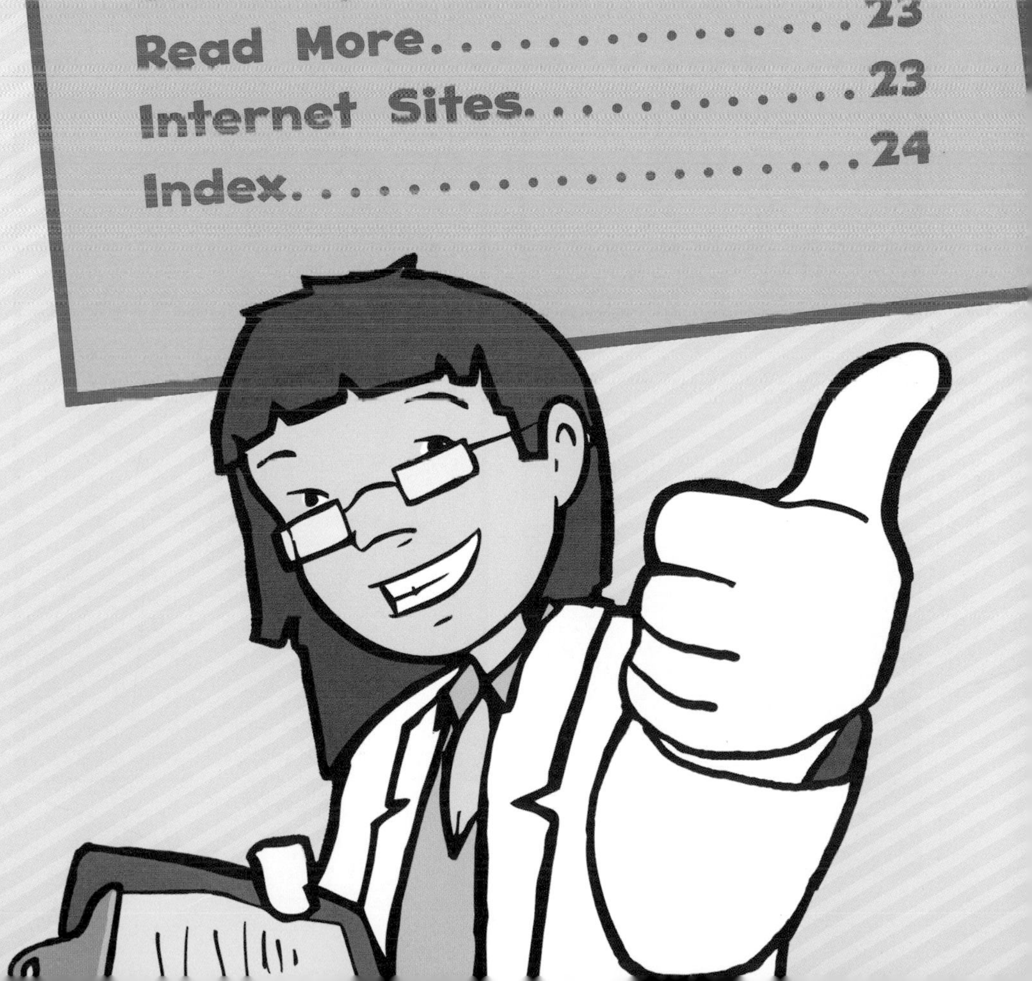

GOT TEETH?

Have you ever taken a good look inside your mouth? How many teeth do you see? 10? 12? 14? Do you still have all your baby teeth?

If so, you'll see 10 teeth on top and 10 on the bottom. 10 + 10 = 20

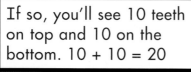

That's a lot of teeth!

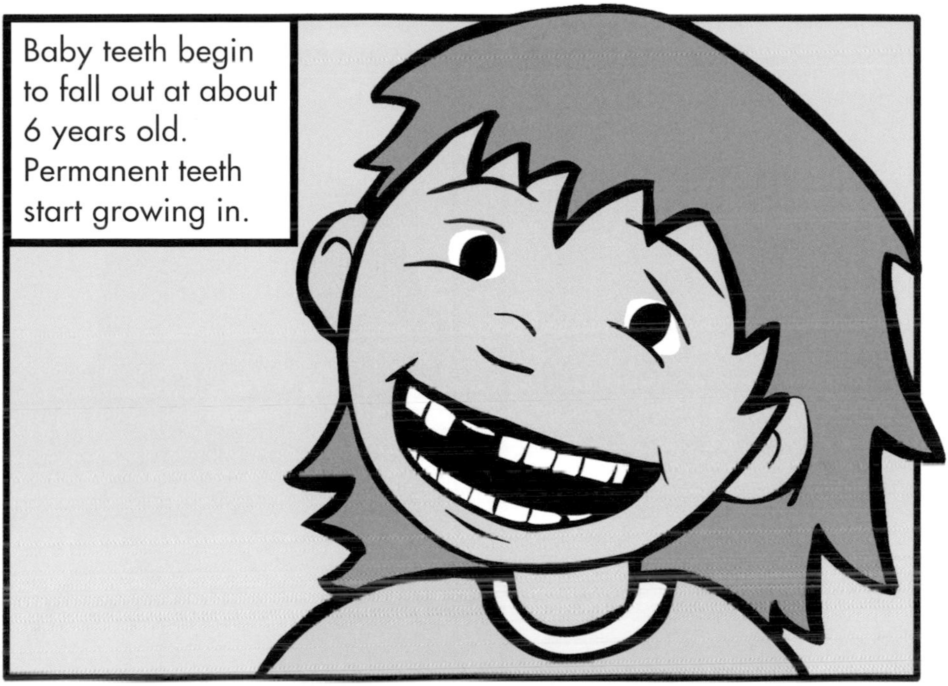
Baby teeth begin to fall out at about 6 years old. Permanent teeth start growing in.

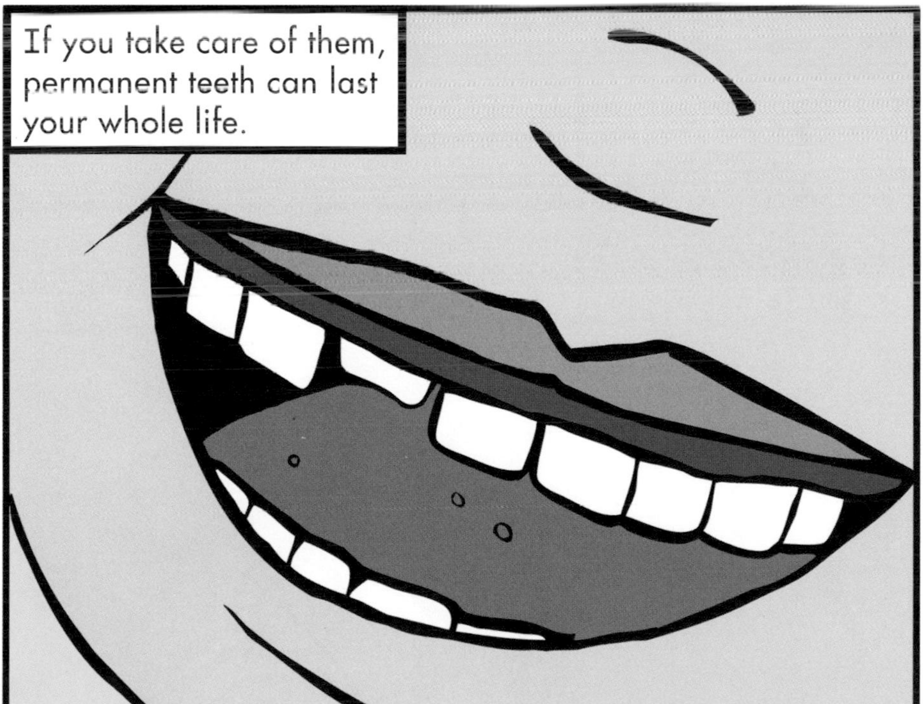
If you take care of them, permanent teeth can last your whole life.

8

The Tooth Exam

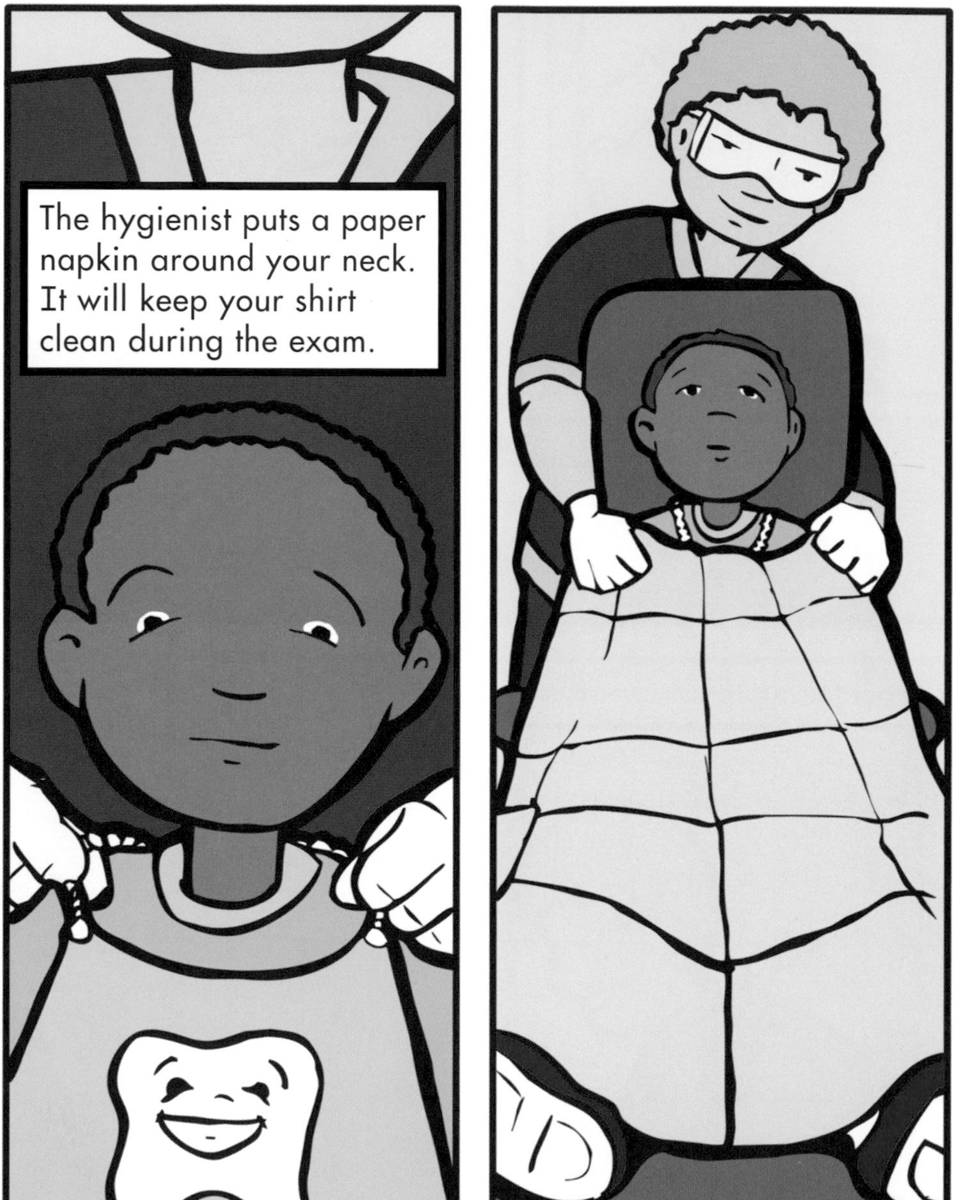
The hygienist puts a paper napkin around your neck. It will keep your shirt clean during the exam.
Then she puts a lead apron on your chest. It's really big and heavy.

The hygienist takes X-rays. She puts a small sensor in your mouth.

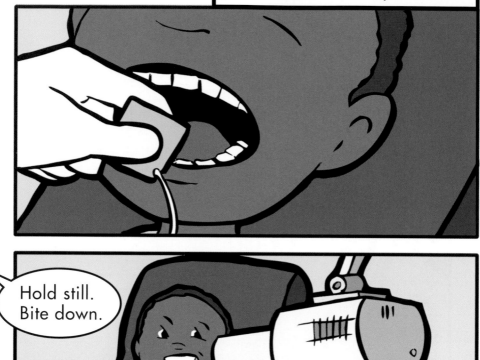

Hold still. Bite down.

CLICK!

That's it.

Hey, that was easy.

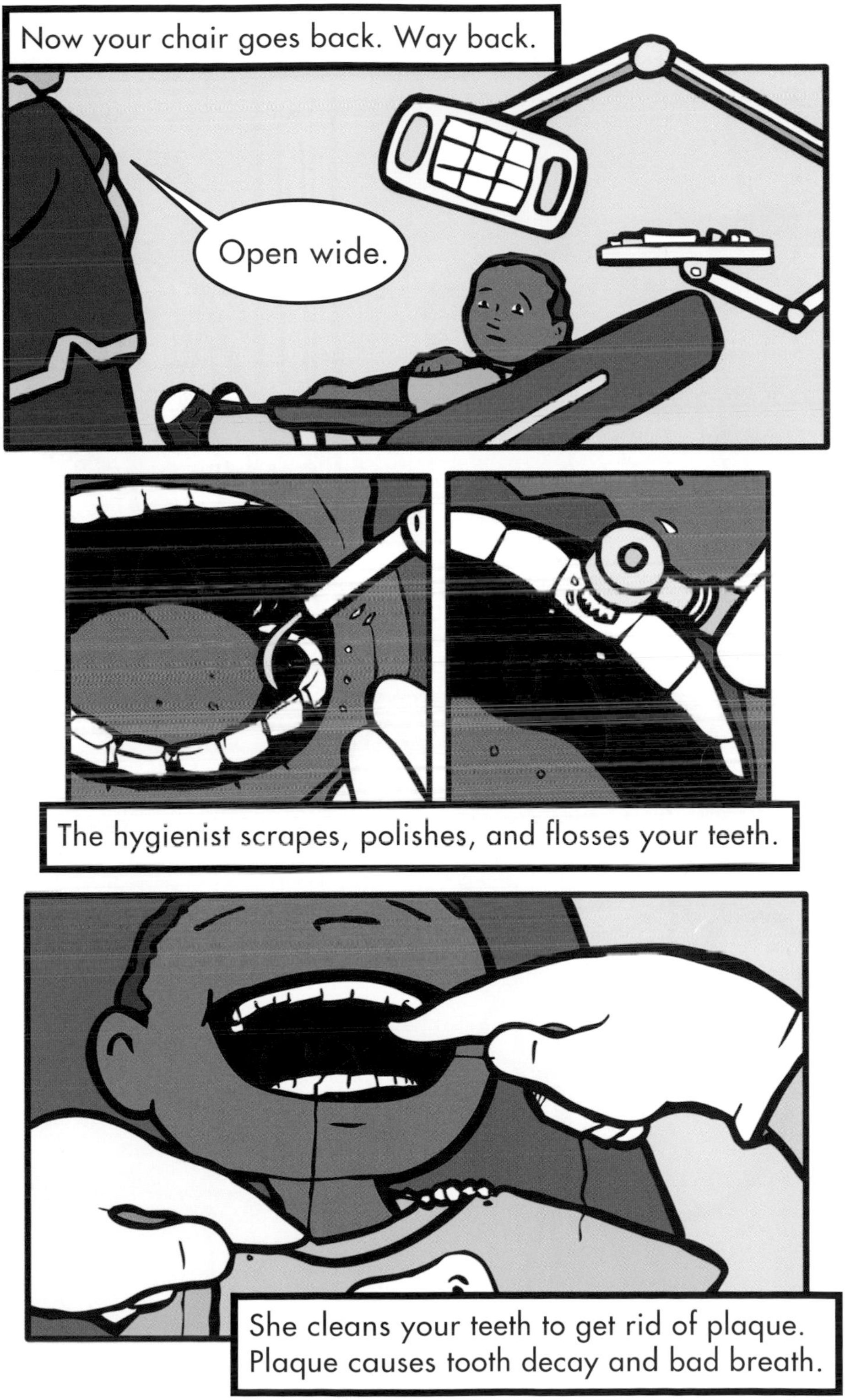
Now your chair goes back. Way back.
Open wide.
The hygienist scrapes, polishes, and flosses your teeth.
She cleans your teeth to get rid of plaque. Plaque causes tooth decay and bad breath.

The Big Question

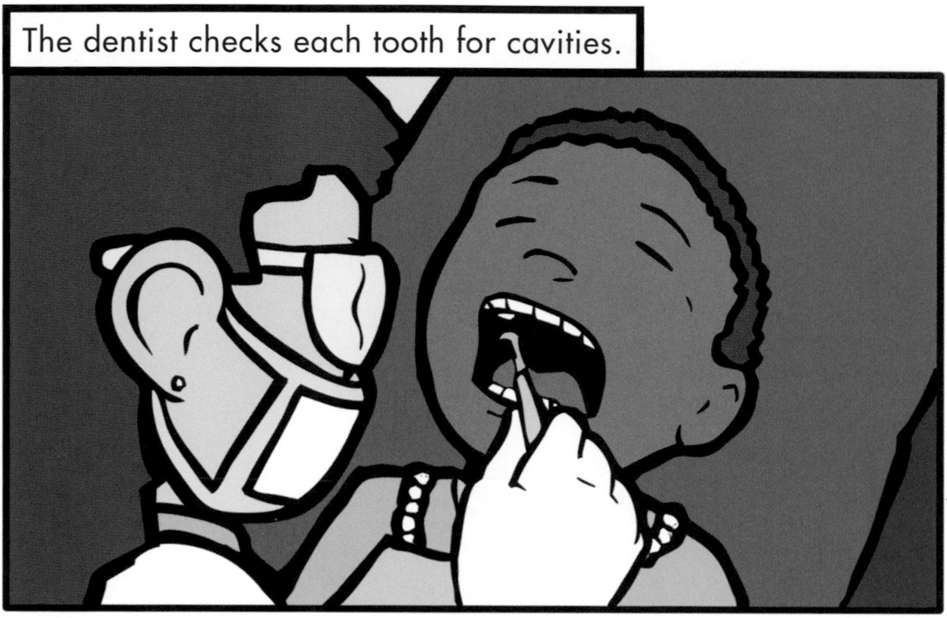
The dentist checks each tooth for cavities.

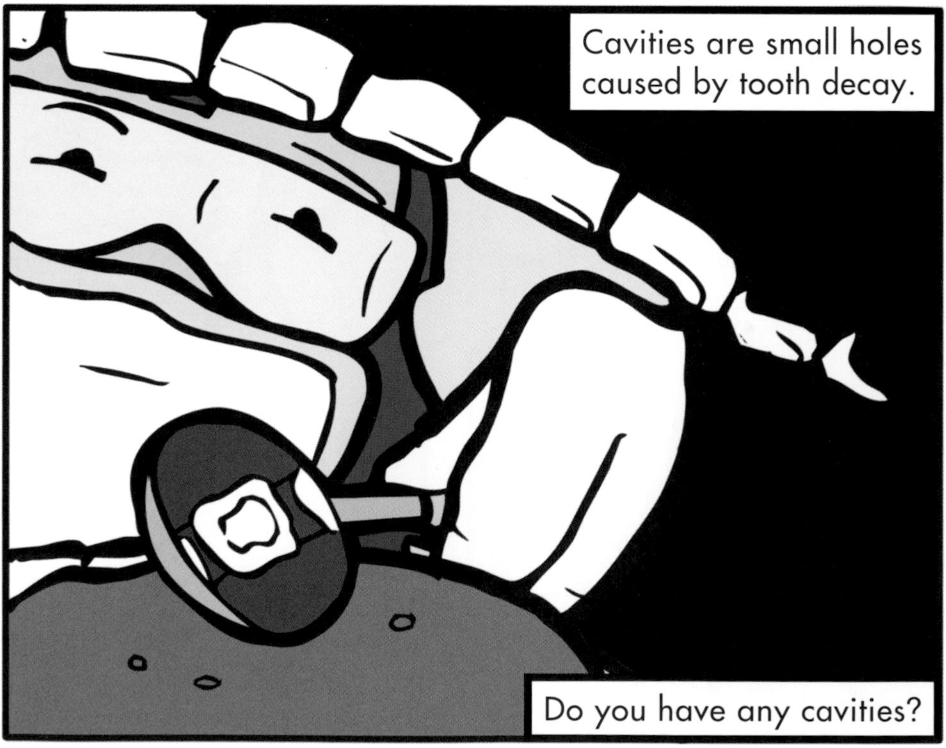
Cavities are small holes caused by tooth decay.
Do you have any cavities?

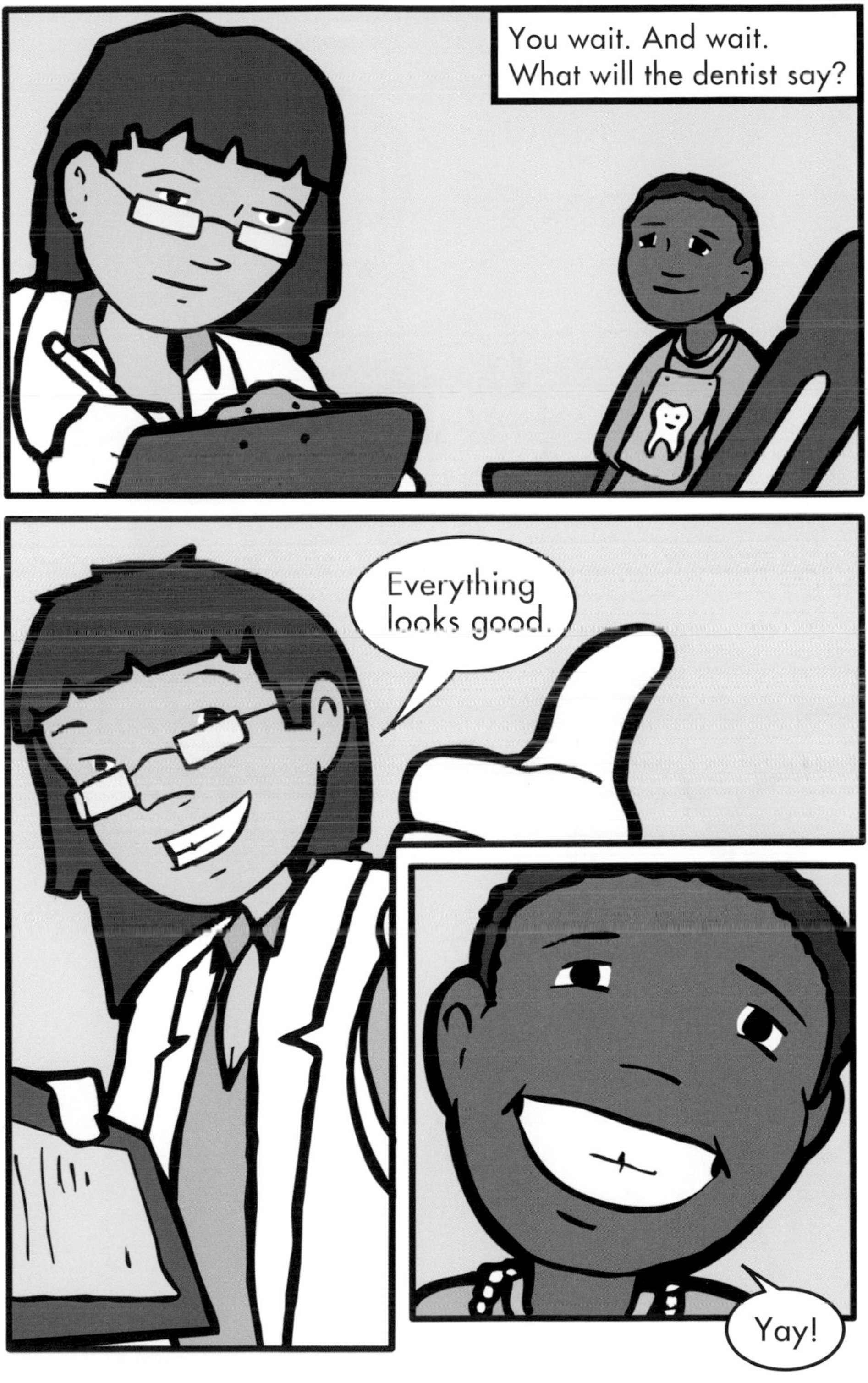
You wait. And wait.
What will the dentist say?
Everything looks good.
Yay!

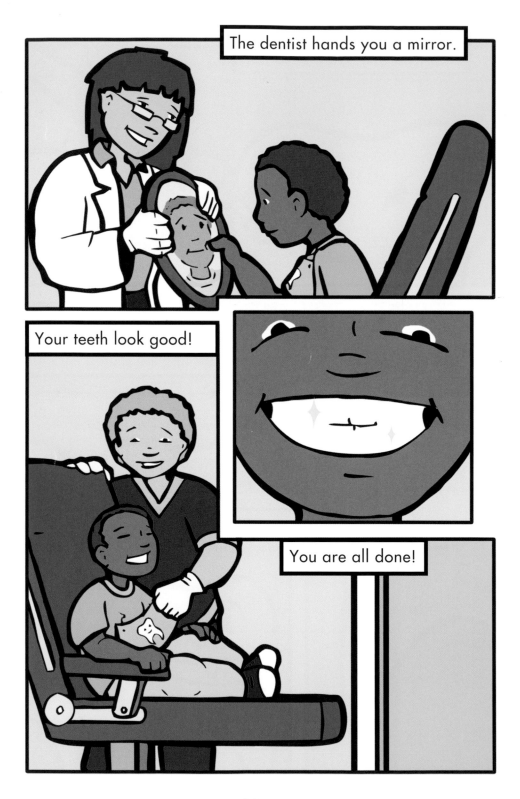

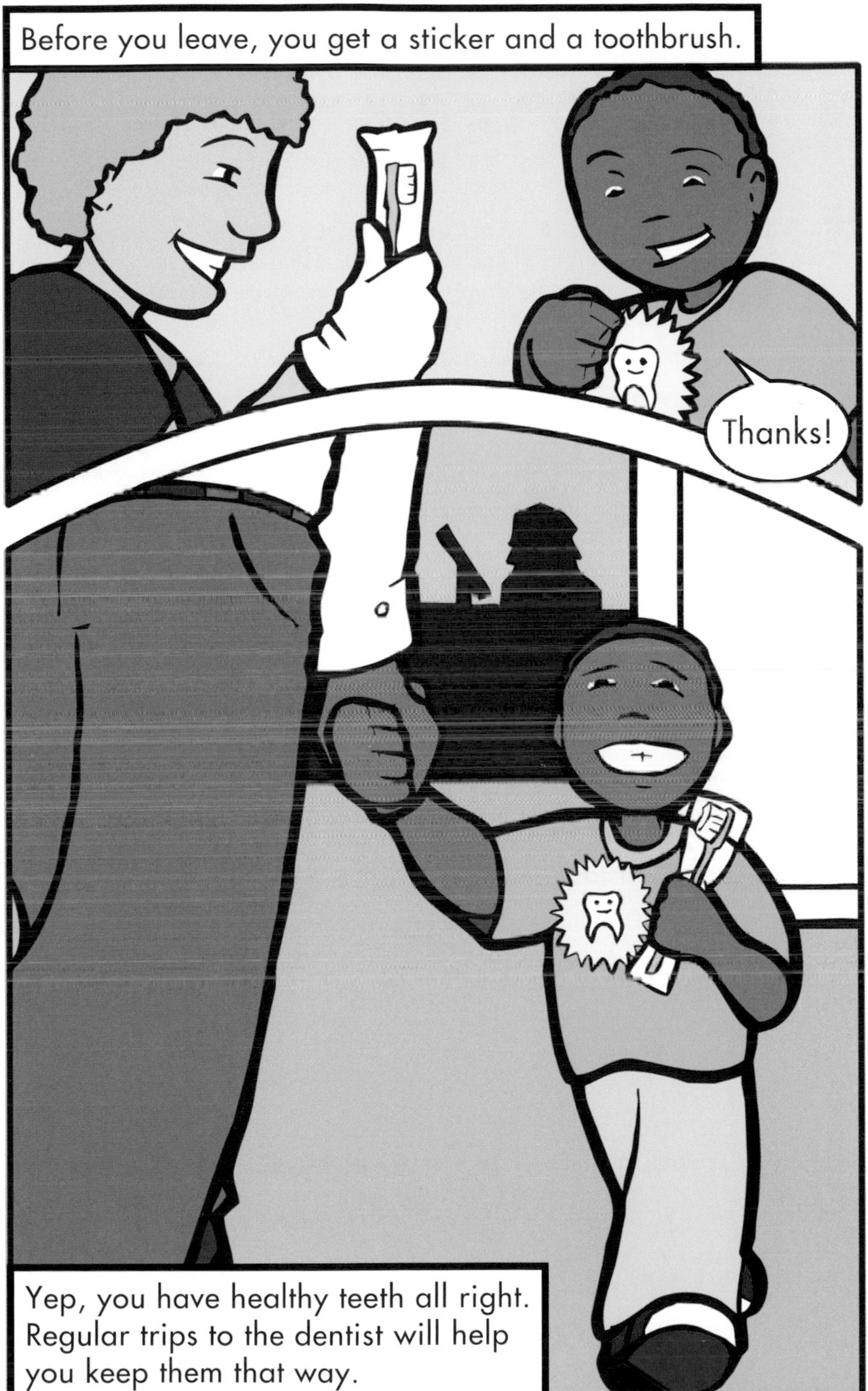
Before you leave, you get a sticker and a toothbrush.
Thanks!
Yep, you have healthy teeth all right. Regular trips to the dentist will help you keep them that way.

GLOSSARY

cavity—a decayed part of a tooth; a dentist takes out the cavity and puts in a filling

decay—rotting or breaking down

dental hygienist—a person who is trained to help a dentist; hygienists clean teeth and take X-rays

filling—matter put into a tooth to stop decay

gums—the firm skin around the base of the tooth

permanent teeth—teeth that grow in after baby teeth fall out

plaque—a thin, sticky layer on teeth that causes tooth decay

sensor—an instrument that can pick up information and send it to a computer

X-ray—a kind of photograph; X-rays can be taken on film or use sensors in the mouth to send digital pictures to a computer; dentists use X-rays to see if a person's teeth, gums, and mouth are healthy

READ MORE

DeGezelle, Terri. *Taking Care of My Teeth*. Keeping Healthy. Mankato, Minn.: Capstone Press, 2006.

Kemper, Bitsy. *Out and About at the Dentist*. Field Trips. Minneapolis: Picture Window Books, 2007.

Thomas, Pat. *Do I Have to Go to the Dentist?: A First Look at Healthy Teeth*. First Look at ... Book. Hauppauge, NY : Barron's, 2008.

INTERNET SITES

FactHound offers a safe, fun way to find Internet sites related to this book. All of the sites on FactHound have been researched by our staff.

Here's all you do:

Visit *www.facthound.com*

FactHound will fetch the best sites for you!

23

INDEX

MY COMMUNITY

TITLES IN THIS SET:

A DAY AT THE
FIRE STATION

GOING TO THE
DENTIST

A VISIT TO THE
VET

WORKING ON THE
FARM